C000131184

FEASTS AND FASTS

FEASTS AND FASTS

VOLUME 1

Edited by
Robert Van de Weyer

Arthur James Ltd

Published in 1995 by Arthur James Ltd.
4 Broadway Road, Evesham, Worcestershire, WR11 6BH

ISBN 0-85305-336-7

Typeset by Little Gidding Books in Bembo.
Printed and bound in Great Britain by Biddles Ltd, Guildford.

PREFACE

The original community at Little Gidding was founded in 1626 by Nicholas Ferrar; their beautiful chapel continues to attract numerous visitors. A new community formed in the late 1970s; and, like its predecessor, it includes families and single people, following a simple rule and pattern of prayer.

Little Gidding Books is the publishing arm of the community. In addition to its Prayer Book it publishes each quarter a book of daily readings, and each year a set of readings and meditations for the festival weeks and Lent. These sets of readings may be used in conjunction with the Prayer Book, or on their own. They are supplied directly to Friends of Little Gidding, and are also available to the wider public through bookshops.

The community is dedicated to Christ the Sower; hence its symbol is a cross made from ears of corn. The hand in which 'Little Gidding Books' is written on the cover is that of Nicholas Ferrar — the words have been taken from his letters.

If you would like to have more information, please write to:

The Community of Christ the Sower
Little Gidding
Huntingdon
PE17 5RJ
United Kingdom

CONTENTS

INTRODUCTION

The first part of this book gives daily readings for the weeks surrounding the major festivals of the Christian calendar: Christmas, Holy Week, Easter and Pentecost. They can be used on their own, or in conjunction with the Little Gidding Prayer Book. They may also be helpful for those arranging special services at these times.

The second part is a course of meditations for the season of Lent; the theme is 'Spiritual Gifts'. Individuals may use this course on their own; and it may also form the basis of weekly group meetings. The meditations are interactive, in that individuals are encouraged to write down their own response to each meditation; and these responses can be shared in a group.

This is the first book in this form. It is hoped that a similar book will be produced each year.

Robert Van de Weyer

FESTIVAL READINGS

CHRISTMAS

December 22

Gradually there gathered the feeling of expectation. Christmas was coming. In the shed, at nights, a secret candle was burning, a sound of veiled voices was heard. The boys were learning the old mystery play of St George and Beelzebub. Twice a week, by lamplight, there was choir practice in the church, for the learning of old carols Brangwen wanted to hear. The girls went to these practices. Everywhere was a sense of mystery and rousedness. Everybody was preparing for something.

The time came near, the girls were decorating the church, with cold fingers binding holly and fir and yew about the pillars, till a new spirit was in the church, the stone broke out into dark, rich leaf, and cold flowers rose to blossom in the dim, mystic atmosphere. Ursula must weave mistletoe over the door, and over the screen, and hang a silver dove from a sprig of yew, till dusk came down, and the church was like a grove.

The expectation grew more tense. The star was risen into the sky, the songs, the carols were ready to hail it. The star was the sign in the sky. Earth too should give a sign. As evening drew on, hearts beat fast with anticipation, hands were full of ready gifts. There were the tremulously expectant words of the church service, the night was past and the morning was come, the gifts were given and received, joy and peace made a flapping of wings in each heart, there was a great burst of carols, the Peace of the World had dawned, strife had passed away, every hand was linked in hand, every heart was singing.

D.H. Lawrence (1885–1930)

December 23

As Joseph and Mary were a-walking the green,
There were apples and cherries aplenty to be seen.

And then Mary said to Joseph, so meek and so mild:
Gather me some cherries, Joseph, for I am with child.

Then Joseph said to Mary so rough and unkind:
Let the daddy of the baby get the cherries for thine.

Then the baby spoke out of its mother's womb:
Bow down you lofty cherry trees, let my mammy have
                                                            some.

Then the cherry tree bent and it bowed like a bow,
So that Mary picked cherries from the uppermost bough.

Then Joseph took Mary all on his left knee,
Saying: What have I done? Lord have mercy on me.

Then Joseph took Mary all on his right knee,
Saying: O my little Saviour, when your birthday shall be,
The hills and high mountains shall bow unto thee.

Then the baby spoke out of its mother's womb:
On old Christmas morning my birthday shall be,
When the hills and high mountains shall bow unto me.

Appalachian Folk Song

December 24

Think of yourself not as an adult, but as a child; not as a large child, but as a tiny baby who has just been born. Imagine yourself lying in a bed of hay, in a manger in the centre of a stable. Your young mother is looking down at you; and your tiny ears can hear the sounds of animals, cattle and donkeys, nearby. Your body is warm, wrapped in soft swaddling-clothes.

The hay is the mercy of God: knowing that God forgives all your sins, you can trust in him and rest on him without fear. Your mother is God's Spirit, watching over you, protecting you and guiding you. The animals represent God's wonderful creation, and the gentle sounds which you hear remind you of the beauty of all God has made. The swaddling-clothes are God's love, which surrounds you, cherishes you, strengthens you, and comforts you.

In the distance you can hear a choir of angels. They are God's truth, proclaiming to mankind the fullness of his mercy, of his Spirit, of his beauty and of his love. Listen to their song, learn its words and its melody, and sing it yourself day by day.

Clare of Assisi (1194–1253)

Christmas Day

Where is this stupendous stranger?
    Swains of Solyma, advise;
Lead me to my Master's manger,
    Show me where my Saviour lies.

O Most Mighty! O Most Holy!
    Far beyond the seraph's thought,
Art thou then so mean and lowly
    As unheeded prophets taught?

O the magnitude of meekness!
    Worth from worth immortal sprung;
O the strength of infant weakness,
    If eternal is so young!

If so young and thus eternal,
    Michael tune the shepherd's reed,
Where the scenes are ever vernal,
    And the loves be love indeed!

Nature's decorations glisten
    Far above their usual trim;
Birds on box and laurel listen,
    As so near the cherubs hymn.

God all-bounteous, all-creative,
    Whom no ills from good dissuade,
Is incarnate, and a native
    Of the very world he made.

Christopher Smart (1722–71)

December 26

So, stick up ivy and the bays,
And then restore the heathen ways.
Green will remind you of the spring,
Though this great day denies the thing;
And mortifies the earth, and all
But your wild revels, and loose hall.
Could you wear flowers, and roses strow
Blushing upon your breast's warm snow,
That very dress your lightness will
Rebuke, and wither at the ill.
The brightness of this day we owe
Not unto music, masque, nor show;
Nor gallant furniture, nor plate,
But to the manger's mean estate.
His life while here, as well as birth,
Was but a check to pomp and mirth;
And all man's greatness you may see
Condemned by his humility.
Then leave your open house and noise,
To welcome him with holy joys,
And the poor shepherds' watchfulness;
Whom light and hymns from heaven did bless.
What you abound with cast abroad
To those that want, and ease your load.
Who empties thus will bring more in;
But riot is both loss and sin.
Dress finely what comes not in sight,
And then you keep your Christmas right!

Henry Vaughan (1622–95)

December 27

But art thou come, dear Saviour? Hath thy love
Thus made thee stoop, and leave thy throne above
The lofty heavens, and thus thyself to dress
In dust to visit mortals? Could no less
A condescension serve? And after all,
The mean reception of a cratch and stall?
Dear Lord, I'll fetch thee thence; I have a room.
'Tis poor, but 'tis my best, if thou wilt come
Within so small a cell, where I would fain
Mine and the world's Redeemer entertain.
I mean my heart; 'tis sluttish, I confess,
And will not mend thy lodging, Lord, unless
Thou send before thy harbinger, I mean
Thy pure and purging grace, to make it clean
And sweep its nasty corners; then I'll try
To wash it also with a weeping eye;
And when 'tis swept and washed, I then will go
And, with thy leave, I'll fetch some flowers that grow
In thine own garden, faith and love to thee;
With those I'll dress it up; and these shall be
My rosemary and bays; yet when my best
Is done, the room's not fit for such a guest,
But here's the cure; thy presence, Lord, alone
Will make a stall a court, a cratch a throne.

Matthew Hale (1609–76)

December 28

Listen, lordings, both old and young,
How this rose began to spring,
Such a rose to my liking,
    In all this world know I none.

The angel came from heaven's tower,
To greet Mary with great honour,
And said she should bear the flower
    That should break the fiend's bond.

The flower sprang in high Bethlehem,
That is both bright and sheen;
The rose is Mary, heaven's queen,
    Out of her the blossom sprung.

The first branch is full of might,
That sprang on Christmas night,
The star shone over Bethlehem bright
    That is both broad and long.

The second branch sprang down to hell,
The fiend's power down to fell;
Therein no soul might dwell —
    Blessèd be the time the rose sprung!

The third branch is good and sweet,
It sprang to heaven, crop and root.
There to dwell and do us good,
    Every day it shows in the priest's hand.

Pray me to her with great honour,
She that bore the blessèd flower,
May she be our help and our succour,
    And shield us from the fiend's bond.

Anonymous

HOLY WEEK

Palm Sunday

In his one hand are pearls;
    A sword is in the other —
        He that now thy door has broken.

He came not to beg
    But out of strife and conquest
    Thy soul to bear away —
        He that now thy door has broken.

Along the road of Death
    Into thy life he came —
        He that now thy door has broken.

Never will he go with half!
    Of all thou art he will
    Be absolute, sole Lord! —
        He that now thy door has broken.

Rabindranath Tagore (1861–1941)

Holy Monday

I was angry with my friend:
I told my wrath, my wrath did end.
I was angry with my foe:
I told it not, my wrath did grow.

And I watered it in fears,
Night and morning with my tears;
And I sunned it with smiles,
And with soft deceitful wiles.

And it grew both day and night,
Till it bore an apple bright;
And my foe beheld it shine,
And he knew that it was mine,

And into my garden stole
When the night had veiled the pole:
In the morning glad I see
My foe outstretched beneath the tree.

William Blake (1757–1827)

Holy Tuesday

Wilt thou forgive that sin where I begun,
    Which was my sin, though it were done before?
Wilt thou forgive that sin through which I run,
    And do run still, though still I do deplore?
        When thou hast done, thou hast not done,
            For I have more.

Wilt thou forgive that sin which I have won
    Others to sin, and made my sin their door?
Wilt thou forgive that sin which I did shun
    A year, or two, but wallowed in a score.
        When thou hast done, thou hast not done
            For I have more.

I have a sin of fear, that when I have spun
    My last thread, I shall perish on the shore;
But swear by thyself, that at my death thy sun
    Shall shine as he shines now, and heretofore;
        And having done that, thou hast done,
            I fear no more.

John Donne (1572–1631)

Holy Wednesday

If death be just a last long sleep,
Then death were good, men say;
Yet say it knowing naught of sleep
Save light at dawn of day.

For sleep's a blank – a nothingness,
A thing we cannot know;
We can but taste the streams of life
That from its fountain flow.

When day puts off her gorgeous robes,
And darkness veils our sight,
Lest we should see her beauty laid
Upon the couch of night,

We crave for sleep because we hold
A memory of morn,
The rush of life renewed, that with
The birth of day is born.

So weary souls that crave for death,
As sweet and dreamless sleep,
As night when men may cease to war,
And women cease to weep,

Are longing still for life – more life,
Their souls not yet sufficed,
Cry out for God's eternal streams;
They crave not death – but Christ.

G.A. Studdert Kennedy (1883–1929)

Maundy Thursday

If thou shouldst never see my face again
Pray for my soul. More things are wrought by prayer
Than this world dreams of. Wherefore, let thy voice
Rise like a fountain for me night and day.
For what are men better than sheep or goats
That nourish a blind life within the brain,
If, knowing God, they lift not hands of prayer
Both for themselves and those who call them friend?
For so the whole round earth is every way
Bound by gold chains about the feet of God.

Alfred, Lord Tennyson (1809–92)

Good Friday

Our part consists in getting down into the death of Christ; his part is to live out his own life in us, just as the waters spring forth from the fountain. Then we shall know what the apostle meant when he said, 'Christ liveth in me'. Where Christ thus dwells in unhindered activity, there will be steady growth, perpetual freshness and abundant fruitfulness; and the life will be marked by ease and spontaneity, because it will be natural.

From this we see that it is impossible to exaggerate the importance of understanding the meaning of his death. We must see that he not only died 'for sin' but 'unto sin'. In the first of these senses he died alone; we could not die with him. He trod the winepress alone; as the sin-offering he alone became the propitiation for our sins. But in the second we died with him. We must know what it is to be brought into sympathy with him in his death unto sin. Oneness with Christ in that sense is the means of becoming practically separated, not only from sinful desires, but also from the old self-life. And this assimilation to the dying Christ is not an isolated act, but a condition of mind ever to be maintained, and to go on deepening.

Evan Henry Hopkins (1837–1918)

Holy Saturday

Christ to hell he took the way
    With wounds wide and all bloody,
The foul fiends to affray,
    With him he bore the cross of tree.

There where the good souls did indwell,
    They chained the gates, and barred them fast.
Ah now, said Jesus, ye princes fell,
    Open the gates that ever shall last.

Now in my father's name of heaven
    Open the gates against me!
As light of light, and thunder flame
    The gates burst and began to flee.

Ah-ha! said Adam, my God I see,
    He that made me with his hand!
I see, said Noah, whence cometh he
    That saved me both on water and land.

Quoth Beelzebub, I barred full fast
    The gates with lock, chain, bolt and pin,
And with the wind of his word's blast
    They broke up, and he came in.

Adam and Eve with him he took,
    King David, Moses and Solomon,
And harried hell in every nook.
    Within it left he souls none.

Anonymous

EASTER

Easter Sunday

Let us cast the eye of our imagination on to the risen body of Jesus. To the wicked he appears severe and frightening; his resurrection is a living reproach of their sinfulness. But to the righteous he appears beautiful and attractive. The wicked want to flee from him; the righteous are drawn closer. The beauty which the risen Jesus possessed is the same beauty which we are promised if we obey him; all who rise with Christ shall share his radiance.

During his earthly ministry Jesus performed many miracles which proved his supernatural power over creation. By his resurrection he received dominion over the whole earth. Every animal and bird, every plant and insect is now subject to his rule. But he does not rule by force, compelling creatures to obey him. He rules by love, inviting people to follow his way so that they may rise with him to eternal life. He wants all to be saved, but he forces no one. If a person accepts that invitation, and begins to obey the commands of Jesus, then his eyes begin to open to the beauty of Jesus; this makes him even more eager to follow Jesus. Thus through the risen body of Christ righteousness brings its own rewards.

Bonaventure (1221–74)

Easter Monday

All other love is like the moon
That waxes and wanes like the flower of the plain,
Like the flower that faireth and fadeth soon,
As the day that showers and ends in rain.

All other love begins by bliss,
In weep and woe makes its ending,
No other love is for our peace
But that which rests in heaven's King.

Whose love is springing, ever green,
And ever full, without waning;
Whose love is sweet, without pain,
Love without end, a perfect ring.

Anonymous

Easter Tuesday

Morning awakes sublime; glad earth and sky
Smile in the splendour of the day begun.
O'er the broad earth's illumined canopy,
Shade of its Maker's majesty, the sun
Gleams in its living light from cloud to cloud;
Streaks of all colours beautifully run
As if before heaven's gate there hung a shroud
To hide its grand magnificence. O heaven,
Where entrance e'en to thought is disallowed,
To view the glory that this scene is giving
What may blind reason not expect to see,
When in immortal worlds the soul is living
Eternal as its Maker, and as free
To taste the unknowns of eternity?

John Clare (1793–1864)

Easter Wednesday

It is not the critic who counts; not the man who points out how the strong man stumbled, or how the doer of deeds could have done better. The credit belongs to the man who is actually in the arena; whose face is marred by sweat and blood; who strives valiantly; errs and comes short again and again; who knows the great enthusiasms, the great devotions, and spends himself in a worthy cause; who at the best knows in the end the triumph of high achievement; and who at the worst, if he falls at least fails while daring greatly; so that his place shall never be with those cold and timid souls who know neither victory nor defeat.

Theodore Roosevelt (1858–1919)

Easter Thursday

I always thought I should love to grow old, and I find it is even more delightful than I thought. It is so delicious to be done with things, and to feel no need any longer to concern myself much about earthly affairs. I seem on the verge of a most delightful journey to a place of unknown joys and pleasures, and things here seem of so little importance compared to things there, that they have lost most of their interest for me.

I cannot describe the sort of done-with-the-world feeling I have. It is not that I feel as if I was going to die at all, but simply that the world seems to me nothing but a passageway to the real life beyond; and passageways are very unimportant places. It is of very little account what sort of things they contain, or how they are furnished. One just hurries through them to get to the place beyond.

My wants seem to be gradually narrowing down, my personal wants, I mean, and I often think I could be quite content in the poorhouse! I do not know whether this is piety or old age, or a little of each mixed together, but honestly the world and our life in it does seem of too little account to be worth making the least fuss over, when one has such a magnificent prospect close at hand ahead of one; and I am tremendously content to let one activity after another go, and to await quietly and happily the opening of the door at the end of the passageway, that will let me in to my real abiding place. So you may think of me as happy and contented, surrounded with unnumbered blessings.

Hannah Pearsall Smith (1832–1911)

Easter Friday

Still, still with thee, when purple morning breaketh,
When the bird waketh, and the shadows flee;
Fairer than morning, lovelier than daylight,
Dawns the sweet consciousness, I am with thee.

Alone with thee, amid the mystic shadows,
The solemn hush of nature newly born;
Alone with thee in breathless adoration,
In the calm dew and freshness of the morn.

As in the dawning, o'er the waveless ocean,
The image of the morning star doth rest;
So in this stillness, thou beholdest only
Thine image in the waters of my breast.

Still, still with thee! As to each newborn morning
A fresh and solemn splendour still is given;
So does this blessèd consciousness, awaking,
Breathe each day nearness unto thee and heaven.

When sinks the soul, subdued by toil to slumber,
Its closing eye looks up to thee in prayer;
Sweet the repose beneath thy wings o'ershading,
But sweeter still, to wake and find thee there.

So shall it be at last, in that bright morning,
When the soul waketh, and life's shadows flee;
O in that hour, fairer than daylight dawning,
Shall rise the glorious thought – I am with thee!

Harriet Beecher Stowe (1811–96)

Easter Saturday

I place before my inward eyes myself with all that I am –
my body, soul, and all my powers – and I gather round
me all the creatures which God ever created in heaven,
on earth, and in all the elements, each one severally with
its name, whether birds of the air, beasts of the forest,
fishes of the water, leaves and grass of the earth, or the
innumerable sand of the sea, and to these I add all the
little specks of dust which glance in the sunbeams, with
all the little drops of water which ever fell or are falling
from dew, snow or rain, and I wish that each of these had
a sweetly sounding stringed instrument, fashioned from
my heart's inmost blood, striking on which they might
each send up to our dear and gentle God a new and lofty
strain of praise for ever and ever. And then the loving
arms of my soul stretch out and extend themselves
towards the innumerable multitude of all creatures; and
my intention is, just as a free and blithesome leader of a
choir stirs up the singers of his company, even so to turn
them all to good account by inciting them to sing
joyously, and to offer up their hearts to God. 'Sursum
corda.'

Henry Suso (c. 1295–1365)

PENTECOST

Pentecost Sunday

When we pray, 'Come, Holy Ghost, our souls inspire', we had better know what we are about. He will not carry us to easy triumphs and gratifying successes; more probably he will set us some task for God in the full intention that we shall fail, so that others, learning wisdom by our failure, may carry the good cause forward. He may take us through loneliness, desertion by friends, apparent desertion even by God; that was the way Christ went to the Father. He may drive us into the wilderness to be tempted of the devil. He may lead us from the Mount of Transfiguration (if he ever lets us climb it) to the hill that is called the Place of a Skull. For if we invoke him, it must be to help us in doing God's will, not ours. We cannot call upon the

   Creator Spirit, by whose aid
   The world's foundations first were laid

in order to use omnipotence for the supply of our futile pleasures or the success of our futile plans. If we invoke him, we must be ready for the glorious pain of being caught by his power out of our petty orbit into the eternal purposes of the Almighty, in whose onward sweep our lives are as a speck of dust. The soul that is filled with the Spirit must have become purged of all pride or love of ease, all self-complacence and self-reliance; but that soul has found the only real dignity, the only lasting joy. Come then, Great Spirit, come. Convict the world; and convict my timid soul.

William Temple (1881-1944)

Pentecost Monday

Lord, speak to me, that I may speak
In living echoes of thy tone;
As thou hast sought, so let me seek
Thy erring children lost and lone.

O lead me, Lord, that I may lead
The wandering and the wavering feet;
O feed me, Lord, that I may feed
Thy hungering ones with manna sweet.

O strengthen me, that, while I stand
Firm on the rock, and strong in thee,
I may stretch out a loving hand
To wrestlers with the troubled sea.

O fill me with thy fullness, Lord,
Until my very heart o'erflow
In kindling thought and glowing word,
Thy love to tell, thy praise to show.

O use me, Lord, use even me,
Just as thou wilt, and when, and where,
Until thy blessèd face I see,
Thy rest, thy joy, thy glory share.

Frances Ridley Havergal (1836–79)

Pentecost Tuesday

When faith is of the kind that God awakens and creates in the heart, then a man trusts in Christ. He is then so securely founded on Christ that he can hurl defiance at sin, death, hell, the devil and all God's enemies. He fears no ill, however hard and cruel it may prove to be. Such faith which throws itself upon God, whether in life or in death, alone makes a Christian man. It kills the past and reconstitutes us utterly different men in heart, disposition, spirit and in all the faculties. Oh! there is something vital, busy, active, powerful about this faith that simply makes it impossible ever to let up in doing good works. The believer does not stop to ask whether good works are to be done, but is up and at it before the question is put. Faith is a lively, reckless confidence in the grace of God. So it is that a man unforced acquires the will and feels the impulse to do good to everybody, serve everybody and suffer everything for the love and praise of God who has bestowed such grace upon him. Pray to God that he work this faith in you; otherwise you will never, never come by it, feign all that you will, or work all you can.

Martin Luther (1483–1546)

Pentecost Wednesday

Workman of God! O lose not heart,
But learn what God is like,
And, in the darkest battlefield,
Thou shalt know where to strike.

Thrice blest is he to whom is given
The instinct that can tell
That God is on the field when he
Is most invisible.

He hides himself so wondrously,
As though there were no God;
He is least seen when all the powers
Of ill are most abroad.

Ah! God is other than we think;
His ways are far above,
Far beyond reason's height, and reached
Only by childlike love.

Then learn to scorn the praise of men
And learn to lose with God;
For Jesus won the world through shame,
And beckons thee his road.

For right is right, since God is God,
And right the day must win;
To doubt would be disloyalty,
To falter would be sin.

F.W. Faber (1814–63)

Pentecost Thursday

Christ called for faith in himself. He never called for intellectual comprehension. He sent out to preach his gospel men who had not any creed or any intellectual faith, only a dumb sort of faith that Christ was more than man. I believe that he sends me out also to help make a better world. Surely that is not an irrational conceit or sentimental twaddle. Christ says that we must begin with faith, but that we can prove the truth of that faith ourselves.

It is not extraordinary that we must begin with faith. It is natural because we have to begin everything else with faith. Faith is an inherent quality of finiteness. It cannot be foregone. We cannot live without it. We cannot make any progress without it. No faith, no business; no faith, no fun; no faith, no victory.

The faith in Christ upon which I have based my life has given me a light on life's meaning which has satisfied my mind, body and soul. The hope that through faith he would reveal a way of life here which justifies it, has been more than answered; and it seems to me ever more reasonable to hold that it will 'carry on' just as gloriously when we have passed beyond the limits of what material machines can reveal to us.

Wilfred Grenfell (1865–1940)

Pentecost Friday

'He went about doing good.' So we might say in our own age of two or three who have been personally known to us: 'He or she went about doing good.' They are the living witnesses to us of his work. If we observe them we shall see that they did good because they were good – because they lived for others and not for themselves, because they had a higher standard of truth and therefore men could trust them, because their love was deeper and therefore they drew others after them. These are they of whom we read in scripture that they bear the image of Christ until his coming again, and of a few of them that they have borne the image of his sufferings, and to us they are the best interpreters of his life. They too have a hidden strength which is derived from communion with the Unseen; they pass their lives in the service of God, and yet only desire to be thought unprofitable servants. The honours or praises which men sometimes shower upon them are not much to their taste. Their only joy is to do the will of God and to relieve the wants of their brethren. Their only or greatest sorrow is to think of the things which, from inadvertence or necessity, they have been compelled to leave undone. Their way of life has been simple; they have not had much to do with the world; they have not had time to accumulate stores of learning. Sometimes they have seen with superhuman clearness one or two truths of which the world was especially in need. They may have had their trials too – failing health, declining years, the ingratitude of men – but they have endured as seeing him who is invisible.

Benjamin Jowett (1817–93)

Pentecost Saturday

'Who hates his neighbour has not the rights of a child.' And not only has he no rights as a child, he has no 'father'. God is not my father in particular, or any man's father (horrible presumption and madness!). No, he is only father in the sense of father of all, and consequently only my father in so far as he is the father of all. When I hate someone or deny that God is his father – it is not he who loses, but me: for then I have no father.

The man who truly loves his neighbour, therefore loves also his enemy. This distinction, 'friend or enemy', is a difference in the object of love, but love for one's neighbour truly has an object which is without discrimination; the neighbour is the absolutely indistinguishable difference between man and man, or it is the eternal resemblance before God – and the enemy also has this resemblance. We think that it is impossible for a man to love his enemy, alas! for enemies can hardly bear to look at each other. Oh, well, then close your eyes – then the enemy absolutely resembles your neighbour; close your eyes and remember the commandment that 'thou shalt love', then you love – your enemy? No, then you love your neighbour, for you do not see that he is your enemy.

Søren Kierkegaard (1813–55)

LENT MEDITATIONS

INTRODUCTION TO LENT MEDITATIONS

The meditations here are from a wide variety of
Christian sources, on the general theme of 'Spiritual
Gifts'. There is one meditation for each day, from the
Thursday following Ash Wednesday, through to the
Wednesday of Holy Week; they thus cover six weeks.
During each week one aspect of the overall theme is
explored; and the first reading for each week is taken
from the New Testament.

Underneath each meditation is a number of empty
lines. It is suggested that you write down your own
responses and reflections to the meditation; if you need
more space, you could keep a notebook. Do not feel you
need to concur with the meditations; their purpose is to
stimulate your own mind, heart and soul.

At the end of each week – perhaps on the Wednesday
evening – small groups may wish to gather to share their
reflections. These meetings may begin by people reading
out in turn what they have written; there can then be a
general discussion. The meetings may begin with two or
three minutes of silence, followed by the Lord's Prayer,
and end with a similar period of silence and the Grace.
Someone will need to be appointed to act as 'chairman'.

WEEK 1
ONE SPIRIT, MANY GIFTS

1:1

There are many different gifts, but the same Spirit grants them. There are many different ways of serving, but the same Lord is served. There are many different forms of activity, but in every activity and in every person the same God is at work. In each of us the Spirit is present for the good of all. The Spirit gives to one person the ability to speak wisely, to another person the ability to express profound truths. By the same Spirit one person receives faith, another the power to heal, another the power to perform miracles, another the gift of prophecy, another the ability to distinguish true gifts of the Spirit from false gifts. Yet another receives the ability to speak in strange tongues, and another the ability to interpret what is said. All these gifts come from one and the same Spirit, who distributes them as he chooses to each person.

1 Corinthians 12.4–11

Some animals like to live in herds, and some animals like to live alone. Human beings in general like to live in herds. One reason for living in herds is the same for both animals and humans: that herds afford protection against enemies, and efficiency in finding food. But human beings have a further, more important reason for living in herds. We are spiritual creatures. We need to love one another and to serve one another. We need to guide one another in loving and serving God. And for this purpose we need one another's spiritual gifts. If there were only one spiritual gift, and each person possessed it, a person could live alone, and guide himself towards God. But there are many gifts, and each person possesses only one or two. So for the sake of our immortal souls we need one another.

Basil the Great (329–79)

We are inclined to divide people according to those who possess spiritual gifts and those who possess material gifts. Thus in our congregations there are those who devote most of their time to spiritual ministries, such as preaching, evangelism and counsel; and there are those – the majority – whose daily work is entirely material. Yet this division is false. When God created the world, he brought the spiritual and material realms together in unity. So too in every person there are spiritual gifts and material gifts. Each person should use both kinds of gifts in the service of others. And a congregation will only flourish if the spiritual gifts which God has bestowed on every member are brought into the service of all.

John Chrysostom (c. 347–407)

Just as every kind of gem becomes brighter and more sparkling when cast in honey, so people seem to sparkle and radiate spiritual light when they are set in the context of their vocation. If a person is called to preach God's truth, then his whole demeanour brightens when he begins to preach. If a person is called to be a confessor, advising and guiding people, he glows with wisdom when people come to him seeking counsel. This is how we discern people's spiritual gifts. A person may attempt to perform various spiritual tasks in God's service; when he radiates spiritual light, we know that he is doing the task to which God has called him.

Francis de Sales (1567–1622)

It is good to put a name to the spiritual gift you possess. A man who has the gift of mending shoes calls himself a cobbler; so when people need their shoes mended, they go to him. The man who has the skill of making furniture calls himself a joiner; so people come to him when they need furniture. If such people were so modest about their skills that they did not name them, their skills would remain unused and wasted. Similarly if you have the gift of teaching, call yourself a teacher, so people will come to you when they wish to learn. If you have the gift of counsel, call yourself a counsellor, so people will come to you seeking advice. Far from being a virtue, modesty about your spiritual gifts is an affront to God, since he bestowed those gifts upon you.

Augustine of Hippo (354–430)

I have one thing to say to you concerning spiritual gifts: exercise these with humility. God has bestowed gifts on you, not so that you can regard yourself as superior to others, but so that you can serve others. How can you learn humility? Two things combined teach humility. The first is an awareness of the huge gulf which separates your state from the perfection of God. This gulf is so huge that you are little better than the vilest sinner; in proportion to the total size, the gulf between sainthood and God is only slightly narrower than that between sinfulness and God. The second is an awareness of the presence of God in every person, object and event. He alone can turn a sinner into a saint; your gift is a tool he has created for himself for this purpose.

Fénelon (1651–1715)

Spiritual ministry of any kind depends on disinterest. The person attempting to minister to others must not be seeking any kind of reward for himself, either in the present or in the future. He must not desire gratitude from others, nor their friendship; he must not look for any particular pleasure or joy in what he is doing. This is not to say that we receive no benefit from ministering to others. Often a person will receive praise and gratitude; a firm friendship will be created; he will enjoy serving others. But if the desire for these things forms any part of his motive, his ministry will be flawed.

John of the Cross (1542–1591)

WEEK 2
PASTORSHIP

As an elder myself, I appeal to the elders of your community. I am a witness of Christ's sufferings, and will share the glory that is to be revealed. I urge you to care for the flock of which God has made you shepherd. Serve them not out of duty, but with a willing heart, as God wants; and work not for money, but out of genuine devotion. Do not give orders to those in your charge, but guide your flock by your own example. So when the chief Shepherd appears, you will receive a crown that never fades.

In the same way, the younger people should give respect to the older; and you should all serve one another wearing humility as an apron. Humble yourselves under God's mighty hand, so that in due time he will lift you up.

1 Peter 5.1–5a, 6

We do not need ever to make decisions; rather we need to discern decisions already made. God has a plan for each of us; at every moment of every day he has decided what he wants us to do. Our task is to perceive his plan and obey it. For this we need help. We need people whose gift it is to enable us to hear God's voice, to attune ourselves to his secret whisperings in our hearts. In truth there are two kinds of people we need. The first are those who can help each individual alone. The second are those who can help congregations, groups, communities. God's plan for each individual is part of his plan for each community; and we must discern his plan at both levels.

Jan van Ruysbroeck (1293–1381)

As a young man I used to attend the regular meetings at our village church, where matters of common interest were discussed. The priest presided at these meetings. He was a good, even a holy man; but he could not guide or lead the people. All sorts of ideas were expressed, and proposals put forward, some good, some bad, and some containing a few grains of goodness amidst the chaff. But the priest could not listen to these ideas and proposals, and then grind and bake them into a cake that would nourish everyone. So they remained like crumbs scattered on the floor. By watching a person who lacked this gift of leadership, I realized that I possessed it and I decided to become a pastor myself. As a pastor I have never had any grand ideas about my status; I just see myself as a baker of other people's ideas and insights.

Michael Ratushany (c. 1825–c. 1875)

Those who have authority over others, as shepherds over their flock, must above all be honest.

They may be tempted to lie in order not to hurt people; so they may imagine that in lying they are doing God's work. But once people realize that they are capable of lying, they will not know which of their words to believe and which not to believe. So even a single lie can destroy their authority. Moreover, while the motive for a lie may be good, the effect is to take away the hearer's freedom. The pastor telling the lie is determining how the hearer thinks, feels and responds; and no pastor has this right over others. If a pastor feels that a person is not ready to hear the truth on some particular matter, it is better that the pastor remains silent.

Eusebius (c. 283–371)

A pastor may court popularity by saying to people what they want to hear. In a congregation where the Spirit is alive and active, most of the pastor's words will indeed be welcome to the ears of the people. He will praise them for their devotion, thank them for their acts of charity, and thence encourage them to be even more devoted and charitable in the future. But even in a good congregation there will be times when people defy or ignore the promptings of the Spirit. And at times the mood of the entire congregation may become fractious and unloving. On these occasions the pastor must make himself indifferent to the opinions of people, and blind to rank and status. He must speak the truth with a demeanour of firm conviction, admonishing people for their sins and urging them to open their hearts again to the Spirit. Initially some will hate and vilify him; but ultimately his people will respect him and thank God for his courage.

Gregory the Great (c. 540–604)

Why has God put this yoke on my neck? I am like the wildest and ugliest horse in the stable; I am a sinner who cannot resist temptation. There are far fitter and more handsome horses he could have chosen; people who are truly good and can control themselves. Yet he has chosen me. I pray that this yoke will control my behaviour so that I shall be an example to my people. And I pray too that they will always remember how sinful I once was, and that, but for this yoke, I should still be no better. Thus they will know that the guidance I offer to them comes not from me, but from God.

Paulinus of Nola (353–431)

A wise pastor cannot make an evil person good, or an evil congregation good; he can only draw out the good that is already there. Equally a foolish pastor cannot turn a good person into an evil one nor a good congregation into an evil one; he can only draw out the evil that is already there. This demonstrates the limits of a pastor's spiritual power. But it also demonstrates the extent of his power. In every person and every congregation there are good elements and evil elements. By drawing out the good elements, the wise pastor enables good to triumph over evil. And by drawing out the evil elements, the foolish pastor enables evil to triumph over good. Thus a foolish pastor should be rooted out as soon as his folly is discerned, and given a less central role. A wise pastor should be respected as a mighty oak tree standing in the middle of a garden.

Catherine of Siena (1347–80)

WEEK 3
TEACHING AND PREACHING

You are the people of God; he loves you and he chose you for his own. So clothe yourselves with the garments that suit God's people: compassion, kindness, humility, gentleness and patience. Be tolerant with one another, and forgive one another whenever one of you has cause for complaint. Forgive one another as the Lord has forgiven you. Above all these garments put on love, which binds everything together in perfect unity.

Let the peace of Christ, which called you to be members of a single body, guide your decisions. Always be thankful. Let the gospel of Christ in all its richness live in your hearts; and instruct one another with all the wisdom it gives you. With psalms and hymns and spiritual songs, sing from the heart in gratitude to God. Let every word and action, everything you do, be in the name of the Lord Jesus, giving thanks through him to God the Father.

Colossians 3.12–17

God has given each person two physical ears; he has also given each person two spiritual ears. When you are listening to a Christian teacher, both your physical ears will be hearing the words he utters. But spiritually let only one ear listen to the teacher, and direct the other ear towards God. As one ear hears the words being spoken, let God through the other ear sift out the truth contained in those words. What the teacher says is inevitably imperfect, because the teacher is fallible. But within that imperfection is to be found nuggets of perfect truth. Likewise the teacher should not ask or expect the full attention of his listeners. He should encourage them to pray as he teaches, so that one spiritual ear is indeed listening to God.

Gregory of Nazianzus (c. 329–89)

To be a teacher or preacher a person must have the gift of eloquence. But this is not enough. Far more important is a soul which radiates the truth. There are many wise people whose souls understand much of the truth which God revealed in Jesus Christ; yet their knowledge is private and personal, so others cannot see and feel it. There are other wise people whose knowledge is public. When they speak, the words they utter seem to sparkle, and even their skin seems to shine; those in their company can feel a warm light shining upon them. All of us can learn the truth and become wise through study and prayer. But God alone determines who can radiate the truth to others; it is a gift to be prized above gold or jewels.

Bernard of Clairvaux (1090–1153)

I spent many years studying philosophy and theology. My teachers complimented me on my intellectual prowess in these subjects. When I completed my studies, I regarded myself as supremely fit to teach and preach the gospel. But as I went out into the world, preaching to labourers and artisans gathered in church, I found that they could not understand a word I said. So I set aside all that I had learnt, and studied how Jesus taught the crowds. I began to follow his example, telling stories, using images and metaphors from daily life, and encapsulating divine wisdom in simple phrases. Now people could understand what I was saying, and were eager to hear more. And for the first time I too began to comprehend the power of the gospel.

Alphonsus Liguori (1696–1787)

In the past I used to prepare every sermon thoroughly, studying deeply and writing out every word I would say. Similarly I used to prepare thoroughly for every meeting I attended, working out in advance the points I would make. Then I noticed a strange thing. On those occasions when I lacked time to prepare a sermon fully or to prepare my contribution to a meeting, I spoke with greater wisdom and eloquence. I realized that, by lack of preparation, I was depending on the Holy Spirit to speak through me. Today I continue to study deeply and to spend much time in thought; but I do not concentrate on the subjects on which I will be preaching or speaking. Then before a sermon or meeting I spend an hour in silent meditation, allowing the Holy Spirit to fill me.

Peter Julian Eymard (1811–68)

I once heard a sermon that was filled with errors. Afterwards I went to see the preacher, and explained to him his errors. He listened with great care to me, considering each point in turn. At the end he declared that he agreed with almost all I had said, and thanked me warmly for coming to see him. The following week in his sermon he corrected all the errors he had made, and apologized to the congregation for having misled them. Such humility, and thence such willingness to learn from others, made that man the best preacher I have ever heard. Thereafter I went to hear him at every opportunity, and week by week his sermons became more profound, more simple, and more compelling. I did not go to see him again, because I gather he welcomed similar counsel from others. But I regularly sent him some trout as a token of my respect.

Robert Bellarmine (1542–1621)

A sermon or a lecture is no more than an introduction to a particular spiritual issue; a person can only learn a small amount by listening passively to another person speaking. The main means by which spiritual knowledge and wisdom is imparted is by asking and answering questions. Let the teacher ask questions of the pupil, compelling the pupil to think out matters for himself; and then let the teacher correct errors. Let the pupil ask the teacher questions: the act of formulating a question is itself a method of learning; and the master's answer completes the process. There is an extra benefit of this dialogue between teacher and pupil: the teacher learns from the pupil also.

Jean Baptiste de la Salle (1651–1719)

WEEK 4
SPIRITUAL COUNSEL

My brothers and sisters, if one of you is caught doing something wrong, then those of you who live by the Spirit must set that person right; but do it with gentleness. Watch yourselves, that you are not tempted in the same way. Carry one another's burdens, because in doing so you are fulfilling the law of Christ.

Those who imagine themselves important, when they are not, are simply deluding themselves. You should each examine your own conduct, measuring yourself by your own progress, not comparing yourself to others. We each have our own burden to carry.

Galatians 6.1–5

We should analyse the nature of our passions, our temperament and our weaknesses, and choose a spiritual counsellor accordingly. If you are an angry person, do not pick someone who is terrified of anger; pick someone who can receive your anger and absorb it. If you are a proud and arrogant person, pick someone who is tough and unyielding, not gentle and accommodating. If you have sexual feelings which you cannot control, do not pick someone who is celibate, but rather someone who is happily and joyfully married, and so understands how those feelings can be expressed legitimately. If you are greedy, do not choose a fat man who comforts you with good food, but an ascetic who has mastered his appetite. In short, choose a spiritual counsellor who has been weak where you are weak, but has learnt to be strong.

John Climacus (c. 570–649)

The best counsellor is the best friend; and the best friend is the best counsellor. When two people have long been close friends, one is able to speak with total honesty and frankness to the other; and the other is able to hear what is being said. And since they know one another so well, the words spoken are likely to be true and apt. No priest or confessor can ever gain this degree of trust and insight with those who come to him. For this reason close friendship is the greatest spiritual blessing we can enjoy on earth. Let us make full use of this blessing, by becoming spiritual confessors to one another, and guiding one another in the way of Christ.

Aelred of Rievaulx (c. 1110–67)

We imagine ourselves to be rational creatures, controlling our lives by the power of the mind. But in truth the heart is far more powerful than the brain; emotions dominate reason far more often than reason dominates emotion. The task of the counsellor is to reach through a person's mind to the heart, opening an interior path through which God's Spirit can enter; then the Spirit can transform the emotions, directing them away from evil and towards good. A person's mind may fiercely resist the counsellor's efforts, refusing to allow the heart to reveal itself; the mind creates a barrier, preventing emotions expressing themselves openly and honestly. The counsellor must enable the person to see this barrier for what it is, so the person can break it down.

Jordan of Saxony (d. 1237)

Those who give spiritual counsel to others naturally wish to offer comfort and reassurance; and at times that is right. Yet this is not a comfortable world. This world is not our permanent home, but rather a stopping-place on our spiritual journey. Our purpose here is to prepare ourselves for the next stage of our journey, which begins at the very moment the breath leaves the body. Thus we should not allow ourselves to become too comfortable here, lest we simply want to rest and relax. The primary task of the spiritual counsellor is to re-kindle energy for the journey, and zeal for the spiritual preparation which the journey requires.

Ambrose of Milan (340–97)

An old priest used to visit his local prison each day. There were six large cells each containing about twenty men; and he went to one cell per day. He spoke to them all together, always on the same theme: that they should confess their crimes to God. He knew that convicting and punishing a man of crime would not change him; only if he turned honestly to God would he become an honest citizen. He found that if he could persuade one man to make a confession, and thence radiate the peace and joy which such confession brings, the others would want to follow suit. So in some cells everyone confessed, and all were happy; in others no one confessed, and all remained in misery. If any of us has any doubts about the value of confession, let us look at those who regularly confess.

John Bosco (1815–88)

God has implanted the propensity to feel guilt in every human heart, in order to deter people from committing sin. Your primary purpose as a counsellor is to enable people to understand this propensity: to look into their hearts, and discern what thoughts and actions evoke feelings of guilt. By understanding his own propensity for guilt, a person gains two priceless fruits. The first is that he can seek forgiveness for past thoughts and actions about which he feels guilty. Many people carry a burden of guilt, without fully comprehending the nature of the burden; when they understand it, they can lift it off their shoulders, and place it before God. The second is that he can avoid thoughts and actions which cause guilt, and in this way keep on the straight and narrow path that leads to heaven.

Leo the Great (d. 461)

WEEK 5
EVANGELISM AND PROPHECY

Anyone who is united with Christ is a new creation; the old order has gone, the new order has begun. All this has been done by God. He has reconciled us to himself through Christ, and has entrusted us with the task of reconciling the whole human race to himself, no longer keeping an account of people's sins. We are Christ's ambassadors; God himself is making his appeal through us. We implore all people in Christ's name to be reconciled to God. Christ was innocent of sin, yet for our sake God made him a victim of sin, that in union with him we can share his righteousness.

2 Corinthians 5.17–21

The kingdom of God does not belong to the most wise, but to the most loving. Wisdom is a particular gift, which some can acquire and others cannot. Love by contrast is a general gift, which all can possess. Wisdom cannot easily be conveyed from one person to another, because words cannot adequately convey truth. Love by contrast is like a forest fire, leaping from one tree to another; and this fire burns more intensely, and spreads more quickly, with each tree that is caught. Thus a kingdom based on wisdom would always remain small and select. But a kingdom based on love can and will eventually cover the whole earth.

H.F. Amiel (1821–81)

Evangelism is not primarily about proclaiming the gospel; it is about being the gospel. When Jesus walked the earth, his gospel was himself: in his own body and soul people could witness the fullness of God's love. He commissioned his church – the universal church, and each congregation – to be the gospel: the church is his body; and the spirit of divine love which permeates it is in his soul. When Jesus walked the earth, people became his disciples because the words he spoke were exemplified in the person he was. Today when evangelists invite people to become disciples of Christ, they must be able to point to the church as the exemplar of his gospel.

Boniface (c. 675–754)

God calls some people to speak forcefully and clearly against every kind of corruption. Let these people speak publicly against general forms of corruption, such as injustice, deceit, bribery and oppression. Let them speak privately against specific acts of corruption, talking to the individuals who are guilty. But let them never mix private and public speech. If they denounce publicly particular individuals, those individuals can denounce them for injustice – for making accusations without giving the individuals being accused an opportunity to defend themselves. Equally if they talk in generalities in private, the individuals to whom they speak will fail to apply the strictures to themselves. It takes great courage to speak against corruption; and it takes care also.

Francis Xavier (1506–52)

Poor wretch that I was, all the while I was ignorant of Christ, and going about to establish my own righteousness; and had perished therein, had not God in his mercy shown me more of my state of nature. But upon a day the good providence of God called me to Bedford, to work on my calling; and in one of the streets of that town I came where there were three or four women talking about the things of God. Their talk was about a new birth, the work of God on their hearts. And they spoke with such appearance of grace in all they said that they were to me as if they had found a new world. At this my own heart began to tremble, for I saw that in all my thoughts about religion and salvation the new birth did never enter my mind. Therefore I often made it my business to be going again and again into the company of these poor people.

John Bunyan (1628–88)

The prophets of old conveyed their message by speaking to crowds in market squares. They endured the constant risk of violent attack, yet their task was made easier by the response of their listeners, whether hostile or favourable, because this stimulated their heart and mind. I try to convey my message – the message which God has given me – with my pen. As I write I am safe from attack; I sit in comfort without fear. Yet I am lonely. I have no one with whom to argue and debate, no one to invigorate my mind and set my heart racing. The message is exciting, but to commit it to paper is drudgery. I communicate in this way because I can reach far more people. May those who read what I write spare a thought for the labour which I have expended, and pray for me.

Jerome (c. 342–420)

When we speak to others about the gospel, we must be on our guard against overwhelming them with our own passion and enthusiasm. God has made every person free to choose: they may choose to accept the gospel or to reject it. He does not want anyone to be swayed by emotion; faith based on emotion is a house built on sand, because it has not been freely chosen. Our task is simply to present people with the gospel clearly and honestly, ensuring that they understand fully the choice which they must make. The rest is between them and God.

Ignatius of Loyola (1491–1556)

WEEK 6
HEALING

Those among you who are in trouble should pray. Those who are joyful should sing praises. Those who are ill should send for the elders of the church to pray and to anoint them with oil in the name of the Lord. Prayers offered in faith will heal those who are sick; the Lord will restore them to health, and the sins they have committed will be forgiven. Therefore confess your sins to one another, and pray for one another that you may be healed. The prayers of the righteous have a powerful effect.

My friends, if one of you strays from the truth, and another brings him back, you can be sure of this: the person who brings the sinner back from his evil path is rescuing a soul from death and cancelling a multitude of sins.

James 5.13–16, 19–20

I used to think that suffering had no purpose, and that healing was no more than the relief of pain. I have now discovered that suffering and healing are the gateway to love. Through suffering I have come to understand the close kinship of human souls with one another. No sooner have you had your full share of suffering than all those who suffer become intelligible to you. But more than that: your mind clears; circumstances and achievements of people hitherto hidden to you become manifest; and you clearly see what is needful to each. And, by seeing your own needs in relation to the needs of others, you realize that healing consists in responding in love to one another's needs. Healing is the fulfilment of this mutual solidarity; each person contributes to the healing of all.

Nikolai Gogol (1809–52)

Heaven lies within all of us; it lies hidden in me now, and if I will it, it will be revealed to me tomorrow and for all time. And in truth the kingdom of heaven will be for us not a dream, but a living reality, which will recreate us afresh; it will heal our psyches. Yet everywhere today people have ceased to understand that true wholeness is to be found in social solidarity, rather than in isolated individual efforts. One day this terrible individualism will come to an end, and people will understand how they had been destroying their own selves by this unnatural separation. They will wonder why they have sat so long in darkness without seeing the light. Then the Son of Man will be seen in the heavens.

Fyodor Dostoyevsky (1821–81)

Do you want to be made whole? Then let your soul become a mirror from which the light of God is reflected back to himself. At present your soul is like a dark woollen ball: the light of God shines upon it and is absorbed; however brightly the light shines, the soul remains dark. Thus you cannot be transformed by God's light. So how does God want to transform you? He wants you to become a perfect image of himself, a perfect image of his Son Jesus Christ. You cannot achieve this perfection under your own strength, nor by any kind of deliberate plan on your part. The most perfect image of any object is achieved by placing the object in front of a mirror whose glass has been rubbed down to perfect smoothness. Let your soul be rubbed down to perfect smoothness, so it may reflect perfectly God's image.

Meister Eckhart (c. 1260–c. 1328)

A man goes to the sea to fetch water. He takes as much as his vessel will carry; but, however large is the vessel, the sea is no emptier. It is the same with those who have the gift of healing. God's grace is like the sea; however much we take of it, his grace never diminishes. The gift of healing is like a vessel, which is dipped into the sea of God's grace. The divine water can then be poured on to as many people as want and need it, and the vessel replenished as many times as required. So if you possess this gift – if you are a vessel of God's healing grace – do not be sparing in your use of the gift. God will always replenish you.

Louis of Granada (1526–81)

Our time on earth is borrowed time. We have no right to life; earthly life is a loan from God, to be invested in works of goodness and love. We have no right to good health; physical well-being is a further loan from God, over and above the loan of life. So when you fall ill, do not resent your condition. Instead interpret illness as a period when God withdraws that loan, in order to enable you to see how much you depend on him. When a friend or neighbour falls ill, go to visit that person, not in order to sympathize, but in order to bring healing. If you can help your friend or neighbour to trust more fully in God's grace, then the illness will have served its purpose; and in God's way that person will be healed. Strangely the final and greatest healing is death, when God withdraws the loan of earthly life and health, and replaces it with the priceless gift of eternal life.

John of Seville (1495–1550)

6:7

An artist is a healer of the soul. All diseases of the mind stem from the isolation of the spiritual from the material elements of the individual. The body concentrates on itself and its own needs, disregarding the soul. This may lead to sensualism, in which the body indulges itself, or to asceticism, so that the body deprives itself, perhaps imagining that such deprivation is good for the soul. But by focusing on itself alone, the body starves the soul. The artist, however, creates images which are material, and yet which speak of the soul. By concentrating on these images the body finds itself peering into the soul – and the isolation of the one from the other is broken.

John Ruskin (1819–1900)

FORTHCOMING TITLES

THE LITTLE GIDDING PRAYER BOOK

The new edition will contain a pattern of daily, weekly and annual worship for individuals and groups. It will be very easy to use, with a cycle of New Testament readings, and psalms drawn from throughout the Old Testament, printed within. It also provides a context, within daily prayer, to use the books of non-biblical readings which are published each quarter – see below.

THE FIRST MARTYRS
Their Defences and Testimonies

When tried by the Roman authorities, men like Justin, Athenagoras and Polycarp – Christian leaders in the second century – gave brilliant defences of their faith. They also wrote letters from prison which are deeply moving. This book provides an edited and accessible version of these writings.

THE LOST EPISTLES
Advice from the Early Church

Throughout the second century, epistles from great leaders were passed eagerly from church to church. Some of these epistles were eventually included in the canon of scripture, and have been studied by Christians ever since. Others, which had no direct connection with the apostles, were left out; and were soon virtually forgotten except by scholars. Yet they contain wisdom and insight which in places is equal to that of Paul, Peter, James and the rest. This popular edition brings these lost epistles, by such men as Clement and Ignatius, to the general reader.

JOHN CASSIAN
East Meets West

Trained as a monk in the Egyptian desert, John Cassian travelled to western Europe at the time when Rome fell. He founded monasteries in France, which in turn profoundly influenced the Celtic church in Britain and Ireland. His writings call ordinary men and women to the primitive simplicity of the gospel.

EUSEBIUS
The First Christian Historian

Much of our knowledge of the early church comes from the pen of Eusebius, who was an intimate friend of Emperor Constantine early in the fourth century. The stories he relates vibrate with spiritual passion – which at times leads to great heroism, and at times pitches the church into terrible disputes.

JOHN CHRYSOSTOM
The Spirit of Protest

Growing up in the late fourth century when the bishops and clergy were becoming corrupted by wealth and power, John Chrysostom was angered by the gap between church and gospel. He believed that Christians were called to live simply and to serve the poor and the sick – and if necessary take political action in the cause of justice. By popular demand he became Patriarch of Constantinople, but was later driven into exile by his powerful enemies. His sermons are masterpieces of both spiritual and political oratory.